W9-BCA-051

WHAT DEGREE DO I NEED TO PURSUE A CAREER IN BOOKKEEPING & ACCOUNTING?

LAURA LA BELLA

Published in 2015 by The Rosen Publishing Group, Inc.
29 East 21st Street, New York, NY 10010

First Edition

Library of Congress Cataloging-in-Publication Data

La Bella, Laura.
What degree do I need to pursue a career in bookkeeping & accounting?/
Laura La Bella.
    pages cm.—(The right degree for me)
Audience: Grade 7 to 12.
Includes bibliographical references and index.
ISBN 978-1-4777-7861-6 (library bound)
1. Accounting—Study and teaching (Higher) 2. Career development—
Juvenile literature. I. Title.
HF5630.L2495 2015
657.023—dc23

                                                                2014007257

Manufactured in the United States of America

CONTENTS

INTRODUCTION

In 2008, at the height of the financial crisis, it is estimated that American investors lost more than $14 trillion. The causes of the financial meltdown—poor regulation over mortgage lending, a growing housing bubble, and questionable banking practices—all led to a recession from which the American economy struggled to emerge.

But as the banking and finance industry took the biggest hits during this time period, many people where wondering where all the accountants were. Did accountants, the people most responsible for looking after the country's collective purse, fail the American people? Were there signs of the financial collapse that accountants missed? How did they miss the loopholes in regulations that led to the crisis? Did accountants play a role in the crisis, or did the crisis surprise even the most skilled professionals in the industry?

Accounting and bookkeeping are vast fields. Nearly every industry employs accounting professionals to watch over their books and to alert organizations to problems before they occur. With such a wide range of industries employing accountants and bookkeepers,

4

By 2022, there will be an additional 204,600 jobs in the bookkeeping and accounting fields.

the career field is large and encompasses different types of positions that use accounting and bookkeeping skills.

From traditional bookkeeping and accounting positions, such as budget analysts and tax specialists, to emerging career fields like forensic accounting, career opportunities abound for those with an interest in mathematics and the ability to problem solve. These fields are almost always steady in terms of hiring. The U.S. Bureau of Labor Statistics predicts that employment in the bookkeeping and accounting field will grow by 11.4 percent by the year 2022. That means there will always be companies and organizations that need bookkeepers and accountants. From the planning services of a financial analyst as a company looks to the future, to the expertise of a tax specialist to file an organization's annual taxes, to the payroll clerk that makes sure employees are paid accurately and on time, opportunities in the field cover a wide range of topics and vary in their responsibilities.

Depending on your career aspirations, you can enter the field after earning a certificate in bookkeeping or accounting, or you can pursue a two- or four-year degree in an area such as accounting, finance, or mathematics. You'll also learn about specific careers in the field, including the most common responsibilities and duties performed by these professionals as well as educational requirements needed for entry into these career paths.

The following sections provide an introduction to the wide range of careers and opportunities in the bookkeeping and accounting field. If you have an interest in numbers, have top-notch skills in mathematics and problem solving, are highly organized, and have a solid attention to detail, a career in bookkeeping and accounting could be for you.

CHAPTER ONE

What Are Bookkeeping and Accounting?

Bookkeepers and accountants work for all kinds of organizations, from large, international Fortune 500 companies that deal with billions of dollars in annual revenue, to nonprofit organizations with small budgets, to small, local businesses making just a few thousand a year. All of them require bookkeepers and accountants to help keep track of the money coming in and out of their organizations.

Bookkeepers and accountants are the brains behind the day-to-day operations of a company. They monitor the movement of money and make sure bills are paid on time, state and federal taxes are calculated correctly, and financial documents are accurately prepared.

What Do Bookkeepers and Accountants Do?

Bookkeepers and accountants are trained to prepare financial records, documents, and statements for companies and organizations. These documents can range from revenue statements to state and federal tax documents. Their duties and responsibilities can include keeping track of a company's financial information on spreadsheets or in databases, producing reports and income statements, preparing balance sheets, analyzing and reviewing financial records for accuracy, and fixing any errors in financial data.

According to the U.S. Bureau of Labor Statistics, some of most common responsibilities are working with expenditures, receipts, accounts payable and receivable, and profit and loss. The term "expenditures" means the money spent by an organization. "Receipts" represent the revenue coming into a company. "Accounts payable and receivable" covers bills an organization needs to pay and money owed to it. "Profit and loss" gives an overview of the financial health of an organization.

Accountants also analyze the costs of a company's operations. When a company creates

Bookkeeping is a complex job. It requires skill with numbers, attention to detail, and financial analysis.

Bookkeepers and accountants analyze the financial viability of business decisions, such as determining if a new product or service can make money or if changes in technology or business practice will impact productivity.

a new product, an accountant is often involved in determining whether the company can manufacture the product at a reasonable cost and make a profit on its sale. For example, Apple's iPad Air retails for $499 for the 16-gigabyte, Wi-Fi-only model, but it costs only $274 for Apple to manufacture. This leaves Apple with a 45 percent margin of revenue, or $225 profit for each iPad Air it sells.

TOP TEN JOBS FOR BOOKKEEPERS AND ACCOUNTANTS

1. Internal auditors
2. Staff/senior accountants
3. Hedge fund accountants
4. Financial analysts
5. Public accountants
6. Controllers
7. Tax specialists
8. Accounts payable and accounts receivable clerks
9. Credit/collections specialists
10. Payroll clerks

Bookkeepers and accountants also look for ways a company can be more cost conscious. They examine financial records to see where a company can cut back on its spending, or where more profit and revenue can be made. This can include identifying less expensive materials to use in manufacturing products, raising the price of a product, or cutting back on staff.

Auditing is another key area where bookkeepers and accountants spend their time. Auditing is a detailed examination of an organization's finances and its compliance with state and federal laws and regulations. In an audit, an accountant or bookkeeper can uncover discrepancies in an organization's financial records. These can include unpaid expenses, uncalculated or missing revenue, unpaid or mounting debts, and other financial issues that could cause problems for a business.

How Do I Become a Bookkeeper or Accountant?

To become a bookkeeper or accountant, basic knowledge of accounting practices and procedures is necessary. This knowledge can be obtained through certificate programs, two-year degrees, or four-year diploma programs. Each one offers its own value based on your career aspirations and goals.

Certificate programs encompass the basic concepts and principles of bookkeeping and accounting. They introduce students to the field of accounting and bookkeeping. These courses are often stand-alone courses, which means they may not be transferable to a community college or four-year degree program. However, certificate programs are an excellent way to learn the skills needed for entry-level jobs in the field.

An associate's degree is a two-year degree program. Available online or at community colleges, these programs introduce students to the profession with courses in accounting, finance, and mathematics. Most programs also include basic business, computing, and liberal arts courses, such as English or public speaking. These programs delve beyond a basic skill level to provide an intermediate-level understanding of accounting and bookkeeping. Some of the credits from an associate's degree can be used toward a bachelor's degree at a four-year college.

A four-year degree in accounting is designed to provide advanced knowledge of accounting, bookkeeping, finance, and business. These programs, offered both online and at colleges and universities, include courses that cover an in-depth understanding of not just accounting and accounting practices, but also the larger role accountants and bookkeepers play in the business and finance industries. A four-year degree in accounting prepares you for a larger variety of career paths.

Types of Bookkeeping and Accounting Jobs

Bookkeepers and accountants can work in virtually any industry. According to *The Inside Track to Careers in Accounting* by Stan Ross and James Carberry, most bookkeepers and accountants can be found working in one of four areas: public accounting, corporate accounting, government accounting, and nonprofit organizations. While their tasks are similar, each area provides a different working experience.

Public Accounting

Public accounting firms provide a wide range of accounting services to individuals and businesses, which can include auditing, tax planning and preparation, tax filing, and general accounting consulting. Accounting firms can be very small, consisting of just one or two people, or extremely large, with thousands of employees. Public accounting firms can have a wide range of clients, which may include both public and private companies, individuals, or organizations. An accountant or bookkeeper working for a public accounting firm may work with several different types of clients.

Corporate Accounting

In corporate accounting, an accountant or bookkeeper works directly for a company or organization, providing services only to that company. In corporate accounting, an accountant or bookkeeper might work in a

Some small companies may try to do their books on their own, but even they can benefit from a professional accountant or bookkeeper to review receipts for accuracy and ensure the business is financially stable.

specific area, such as auditing, taxes, or mergers and acquisitions. Their work becomes part of the organization's larger, consolidated financial statements and documents, which outline all parts of the organization.

Government Accounting

A vast number of accountants, more than one hundred thousand, according to the U.S. Bureau of Labor Statistics, work for federal government agencies such as the Internal Revenue Service (IRS), the Securities and Exchange Commission (SEC), or the General Accounting Office. Still more work for local and state government offices. In these capacities, bookkeepers and accountants might investigate financial crime committed by businesses and government professionals (white collar crime), manage public funds, perform financial audits, collect taxes, or conduct research.

Nonprofit Organizations

A nonprofit organization is a group that uses its earnings to achieve specific goals for the benefit of a community. Nonprofit organizations provide a wide range of services to the public, which can include civic, religious, social, professional, health and welfare, and educational services. Churches, colleges and universities, and museums are all examples of nonprofit organizations. Bookkeepers and accountants who work for nonprofit organizations have to follow specific regulations regarding the use of revenue and must also file public financial records.

CHAPTER TWO

On the Path to a Career in Bookkeeping and Accounting

There are multiple ways to pursue a career in bookkeeping and accounting. Is a certificate program the right path for you, or is a degree the better option? It all depends on your career goals and aspirations, and what you hope to do as you think about your long-term career.

There are multiple career paths and degree programs for those interested in accounting or bookkeeping professions.

The Right Path: Certificate or Degree?

You have your choice of two educational paths as you consider a career in bookkeeping and accounting.

You can complete a certificate program, or you can enroll in a degree program. Both options provide an understanding of the field and offer employment opportunities upon completion.

Certificate Programs

A certificate program in bookkeeping or accounting is often a set of six to eight courses that cover the basics of the field. You will complete only accounting and accounting-related courses, which give you an overview of the field, teach you to prepare financial documents, and provide a broad understanding of the computing software you will use on a daily basis. You will also learn taxation regulations and licenses, taxation laws, the practices of payroll taxes, business tax return filing, and tax planning.

Pros and Cons of a Certificate Program

A certificate program can:

- Prepare students for entry-level accounting and bookkeeping jobs
- Offer courses online or part-time, which accommodates a student who works full-time or those who want to upgrade their knowledge quickly
- Provide a basic introduction to the field for those who find that their job involves some accounting work

The disadvantages to a certificate program include:

- Curriculum that provides only a glimpse of the accounting field and will not prepare you for more advanced level practices
- Limited exposure to accounting and bookkeeping professionals who can offer you insights on the day-to-day work of accountants or the job search process
- Limited job advancement and earning potential

Degree Programs

There are two types of degree programs for accountants and bookkeepers: associate's degrees and bachelor's degrees. An associate's degree is a two-year program leading to an associate of applied science (AAS) or associate of science (AS) degree. A bachelor's degree

Two and four-year degree programs include a well-rounded education where students learn accounting and bookkeeping fundamentals while they hone their writing, presentation, and communication skills.

is a four-year program leading to a bachelor of science (BS) or bachelor of arts (BA) degree.

Associate's Degree in Accounting and Bookkeeping

An associate's degree is a good choice if you want to enter the workforce more quickly, or it can prepare you for advanced study in a four-year bachelor's degree program. The curriculum includes courses in accounting, business, mathematics, and general education. You will complete introductory and intermediate level accounting courses that provide a deeper understanding of accounting, accounting principles and practices, and the regulatory standards of the field. Business courses provide an overview of economics, business applications, money management, and organizational behavior. These courses give you insight into the role accounting plays in the larger functions of the business environment. Advanced mathematics courses sharpen your math skills. General education courses, often in areas such as English, communications, or public speaking, round out your education and help to hone your interpersonal communication skills. Some two-year programs allow students to select electives, which are courses chosen by the student, in a related subject area. For accounting and bookkeeping, courses in forensic accounting, marketing, or accounting information systems can introduce you to related career paths and provide a basic understanding of these areas.

Pros and Cons of an Associate's Degree

Among the advantages, an associate's degree:

- Is less time intensive. In less than two years, students can complete the degree program and become qualified for a number of challenging entry-level positions.
- Costs less than a four-year degree.
- Prepares you for further education, such as a bachelor's degree.

Among the disadvantages with this degree:

- Students are not as marketable against candidates with a bachelor's degree.
- Graduates' earning potential is lower compared to those with an advanced degree.
- It is difficult to be promoted to managerial or supervisory positions because it is not a four-year degree.

Bachelor's Degree in Bookkeeping and Accounting

A bachelor's degree is a four-year program that prepares you for advanced positions in the field. Professionals with a bachelor's degree can take on more responsibility due to the advanced course work they complete.

A four-year degree includes introductory courses similar to an associate's degree, with the addition of more advanced courses. Students complete higher-level mathematics courses, such as statistics and applied calculus. Advanced accounting courses, in areas such as corporate finance, forensic accounting, fraud examination, internal auditing, small business taxation, and personal taxation, maximize your knowledge of accounting and give you a background in multiple areas of the field. This broader understanding creates more career opportunities and makes you qualified for general accounting positions, as well as jobs in specific subfields of accounting and bookkeeping. You will also complete business courses, such as marketing, operations management, global business, business ethics, organizational behavior, and business strategy. These give you an in-depth look at the business world and its operations both domestically and internationally. They can also help prepare you for leadership or managerial positions.

Nearly all bachelor's degrees require students to complete general education courses, which provide you with a universal foundation in the liberal arts and humanities. In addition, many four-year programs allow you to select a minor or concentration in a secondary area of study. These courses provide you with the opportunity to explore another area of interest related to your accounting or bookkeeping program and give you a second area of expertise.

Pros and Cons of Getting a Bachelor's Degree

A bachelor's degree is the most intensive program of study of the three educational paths. A bachelor's degree:

- Helps to fulfill the educational requirement necessary for a candidate to sit for the certified public accounting (CPA) exam
- Prepares students for graduate study
- Increases graduates' job prospects by making them qualified for a larger number of jobs

Among its disadvantages, a bachelor's degree can be:

- The most costly of the three educational pathways
- Time intensive with four years of school to complete

What Is the Right Program for Me?

You can complete these educational pathways via online programs, community college, and four-year colleges and universities. Each has its own set of opportunities and challenges.

Online programs offer certificate programs and two- and four-year degrees. They are the most flexible in terms of pacing and time. Online courses are convenient: students can complete assignments in their own time frame as long as they meet professors' deadlines. They are a

Online programs may be convenient for those who are working. Students can do coursework on their own schedule.

great way to continue your education if you are already employed full-time, your job requires you to travel, or you are considering a career change. Online courses mean you can log in from virtually anywhere in the world.

But online programs require a certain level of maturity. You must be independent and self-disciplined in completing tasks and posting assignments on time. Quality in online programs varies greatly. You'll want to research online colleges to determine which ones are reputable and will provide the highest quality education. Online programs are not always the less expensive option.

Community colleges offer certificate programs and two-year degrees. They are often more affordable, and some courses can be transferred to four-year programs. There is less flexibility in study options and you are required to attend classes regularly. Many community colleges have an active campus life for their students, which can include sports teams, clubs, and on-campus activities.

Four-year colleges offer bachelor's degrees. They have the most extensive selection of courses from which to choose. There are a wide range of colleges and universities, and each offers its own on-campus experience. Many have sports teams and extensive student clubs and organizations. These extracurricular activities can develop your leadership and management skills, improve your communication skills, and help you develop interests outside of your career path.

The Cost of an Education

Whichever pathway you choose, you will be paying for your education. Certificate programs are the least expensive, followed by two-year programs and four-year programs, which cost the most. Where you choose to study will also affect cost. A private college or university is more expensive than a state-sponsored school. Online programs are not always the less expensive option. The tuition for the University of Phoenix's BS degree in accounting is $62,000 (as of this writing), which includes tuition, course-related materials, and fees. By comparison, the University of Pennsylvania, whose bachelor's degree in accounting tops the *U.S News & World Report* list of Best Undergraduate Accounting

TOP TEN WAYS TO PAY FOR COLLEGE

1. Apply for financial aid.
2. Apply for national grants.
3. Apply for local scholarships.
4. Apply to a wide range of schools with varying tuition rates.
5. Negotiate a better deal by taking one financial aid package to another school to see if it can match or make you a better offer.
6. Find a benefactor, such as the Peace Corps or ROTC, that can help pay for some, if not all, of your college expenses.
7. Explore international schools, where tuition is often lower for U.S. students.
8. Live at home to avoid room, board, and meal plan expenses.
9. Take advantage of the American Opportunity Tax Credit and the Lifetime Learning Credit, which make some of your tuition costs tax deductible.
10. Talk to a guidance counselor at school: they often know of other opportunities or options that can lessen the expense of college.

Programs for 2013–14, costs almost $46,000 for tuition, room and board, and related fees. Smart students will research their options to determine which makes the most financial sense.

What Kind of Financial Aid Is Available?

Many colleges and universities offer scholarships, financial aid, stipends, or work opportunities that help defray the costs of a degree. Scholarships are free money awarded to students who meet various criteria, from high grades to athletic ability. Financial aid is tuition support based on students' personal finances. Many colleges also offer work-study, which requires students to work for the college in exchange for a salary that can be used toward tuition and living expenses.

Community colleges often have "two-plus-two transfer options," whereby students begin at a community college to complete a two-year associate's degree, then transfer to a four-year program (for two years) to earn a bachelor's degree. Splitting the program can cut down on the tuition costs of attending a four-year program from the beginning.

CHAPTER THREE

Tailoring Your Education

The accounting and bookkeeping fields are vast. There is a wide range of jobs from which to choose, including traditional accounting and bookkeeping positions, to emerging subfields such as forensic accounting and accounting information systems. Tailoring your education to meet your career objectives can make the most of your time in school and get you the job you want when you graduate.

How to Get the Education You Want

Many two- and four-year degree programs allow students to choose extra classes in areas outside the required course work. You can select topics of study to enhance your knowledge of the field, develop a

Deciding on a degree program can be confusing, but a college adviser can help.

secondary area of expertise in a related field, or develop an outside interest.

Elective courses are classes students can choose from a selection of alternative courses in their area of study. Many programs offer students electives in additional areas of accounting or in business. Courses such as federal taxation, economics, marketing, or management could be among the electives available, based on your program.

A concentration is a set of three to five courses for more in-depth understanding of a subject area. These courses provide an introduction into a secondary field

JEFF THOMSON, PRESIDENT AND CEO OF THE INSTITUTE OF MANAGEMENT ACCOUNTANTS

In a September 2012 interview with *Forbes* business magazine, Jeff Thomson, president and chief executive officer of the Institute of Management Accountants, was asked to name the biggest issue holding back young accounting professionals in the work place. His response: communication and leadership skills. "Taking the initiative to say, 'Hey, I want to be involved in things! How do I work with team members?' It's something not a lot of people are coming out of college with and it's noticeable when you interview students," he said. "Without those basic communication skills, you can struggle as you move up the corporate ladder; it's an important skill."

of study that is both related to accounting and book-keeping and useful for the student. Examples of concentrations include statistics and mathematics.

A minor is a set of about five courses (sometimes more) in a different, often related career field. Minors provide the most depth and breadth in a secondary area of study. Minors go beyond introductory courses and help establish expertise in an area that supports a major, such as communication, finance, management information systems, or business administration management.

The IMA is an international association of accountants and financial professionals. Its annual conference is an event dedicated to education and networking opportunities for its more than sixty-five thousand members.

Real-World Experience: Internships and Cooperative Education

One way to set yourself apart from other job candidates is to obtain real working experience before you graduate. The role of an internship or cooperative education experience (co-op) is to gain real, hands-on experience in accounting and bookkeeping.

There is a difference between an internship and a co-op. Internships are short stints of work in which you observe and learn on the job, usually lasting a few weeks to a few months. You might spend a few hours a week at your internship, completing short tasks or assisting a full-time employee in preparing financial documents and other materials. A co-op is a longer work period, typically a full semester or summer, in which you work full-time under an accounting or bookkeeping supervisor. As a co-op, employers tend to give you more meaningful work assignments and larger pieces of a project. Since co-op work periods are longer, students spend more time on a project, maximize their involvement, gain valuable on-the-job experience, and even witness the outcome of their contributions. Co-ops are paid experiences, which can help offset tuition expenses. Often, internships are unpaid, but students gain college credit.

Many colleges and universities have extensive internship and co-op programs, and some even make these experiences a requirement for graduation. Many schools assist students in identifying opportunities at companies, arranging on-campus interviews, and coordinating leave for students who choose to co-op during the academic year.

Benefits of an Internship or Co-Op

An internship or co-op can become a valuable experience that can lead to your first job in the accounting and bookkeeping field. The benefits of these experiences are many.

Apply Classroom Knowledge

Classroom learning is essential to understanding the concepts and principles of accounting and bookkeeping. But an internship or co-op lets you apply those skills on the job. You'll see how assignments and classroom lectures connect to the field as you use the skills you learned in class and apply them to real-world problems.

Gain Valuable Work Experience and Boost Your Résumé

Most job applicants have similar course work on their résumés. But many employers prefer applicants who have completed an internship or co-op, or have other relevant work experience. In a tight job market, where there could be hundreds of applicants, it's important to set yourself apart from other candidates.

MAKE THE MOST OF AN INTERNSHIP

1. **Show initiative.** Seek out and ask for opportunities to work on exciting projects or be the first to volunteer when a task needs to be completed.

2. **Meet people.** Get to know professionals in other departments, ask about their jobs and responsibilities, and learn how they got started in the field. You'll gain insights into the larger role accounting plays in the company, as well as the other types of careers that work alongside accountants and bookkeepers.

3. **Attend events.** Many internships and co-ops offer networking opportunities, educational seminars, or the chance to attend a professional conference. Don't pass these up. The point of an internship or co-op is to learn as much as you can about the career and the industry as a whole.

4. **Ask for a performance review.** Find out how well you're performing at your internship or co-op by asking for a formal review. These one-on-one sessions with your supervisor can pinpoint any problems with your work, provide you with opportunities to improve your skills, or help you learn from any mistakes you've made.

Prove Your Skills

Internships and co-ops are great ways for a company to witness firsthand what type of employee you will be, if you are capable of doing the work assigned to you, and if you possess the intangible elements the company seeks, such as working hard and taking initiative. Many companies use their internship and co-op programs to scout talent for future jobs.

Network with Professionals

Networking, or meeting and staying in touch with people in your field, is one of the most important ways to land a job. Internships and co-ops give you an opportunity to

Meeting with experienced professionals in the field, as well as alumni from your college or academic program, can help you find a job and gain insight into the accounting and bookkeeping profession.

get to know people who can provide advice and career guidance and become professional references who can speak to your skill and abilities. They might even be in a position to hire interns and co-op participants when positions open up.

Gain Confidence and Maturity

An internship will give you a chance to gain experience that you can talk about on job interviews later. You'll also feel more confident when applying to jobs, knowing that your internships will make you a more marketable and impressive candidate over others with little to no experience. As a bonus, when you are interviewing and you are asked if you know how to do a particular task, you may be able to answer positively based on what you learned during your internship.

CHAPTER FOUR

Accounting, Auditing, or Bookkeeping Clerks

An accounting, auditing, or bookkeeping clerk creates financial records and documents for an organization. These clerks are responsible for keeping track of financial transactions, updating financial statements, producing various types of reports, and checking the accuracy of the information they produce.

Duties and Job Responsibilities

According to the U.S Bureau of Labor Statistics, bookkeeping, accounting, and auditing clerks typically use bookkeeping software, online spreadsheets, and databases to track financial information; post financial transactions into special computer software designed to track financial information; receive cash, checks, and other forms of revenue and record them appropriately; track debits and credits to the correct accounts; produce a wide variety of documents and reports, including balance sheets and income statements that inform company leadership of the financial health of an organization; review financial documents for accuracy, mistakes, or fraud; and reconcile and report any difference discovered during their review.

The three jobs each carry some specific areas of responsibility. According to the National Bookkeepers Association, bookkeepers can only work on financial statements and reports if they have QuickBooks certification. This certification tests a bookkeeper's ability to set up QuickBooks accounts and work with several of the software's key features. The exam consists of fifty multiple-choice questions and simulations that test bookkeepers' skills using the software.

It is the role of an accountant or bookkeeper to keep track of money coming in from purchases (revenue) and going out (expenses).

Depending on the employer, some accounting clerks may find they have a narrow set of tasks, such as focusing on accounts payable or accounts receivable. This will depend on where they work. At a large accounting firm or company, chances are good the clerk will focus on just a few tasks. At smaller operations, they may do the full range of accounting functions.

The main focus of an auditing clerk is on properly coding information in financial statements, reviewing the documents, and communicating any errors, fraudulent behavior, or suspicious activity to accountants or a supervisor.

Educational Requirements

Many accounting, auditing, or bookkeeping clerks need a high school diploma. Strong candidates should have some basic math and computer skills, including knowledge of spreadsheets and the various types of bookkeeping software commonly used. Some employers may prefer to hire a candidate with some postsecondary education, such as a certificate or associate's degree in accounting or bookkeeping.

Many clerks learn the skills they need on the job. A supervisor or training specialist will often work with a new clerk until he or she is proficient in the job's duties and responsibilities. Sometimes a company will suggest some formal training for the clerk so he or she may can master certain skills, such as learning a specific computer software system.

In addition to the QuickBooks certification, there are several other certifications available to accounting, auditing, and bookkeeping clerks. The certified payroll specialist (CPS) license verifies that you possess the knowledge, skill, and experience needed to execute payroll functions. To obtain the CPS license, you must pass an exam, have one year (or two thousand hours) of payroll experience, agree to the CPS Code of Professional Conduct, obtain sixteen hours of certified professional education each year, and submit the CPS application for licensure.

The Microsoft Excel certification tests your competency in Excel, a spreadsheet and database software commonly used in the field. The exam covers creating and editing data, modifying an Excel worksheet, formatting, creating charts, managing large workbooks, creating graphics and screenshots, and utilizing the multiple functions available within the software.

The certified bookkeeper designation requires two years of full-time experience (or equivalent part-time work) and successfully passing a four-part exam, which includes adjusting entries, error correction, payroll, depreciation, inventory and internal controls, and fraud prevention.

TOP U.S. CITIES FOR BOOKKEEPERS

1. New York, New York
2. Houston, Texas
3. Boston, Massachusetts
4. Chicago, Illinois
5. Washington, D.C.
6. Phoenix, Arizona
7. Philadelphia, Pennsylvania
8. Denver, Colorado
9. Minneapolis, Minnesota
10. Seattle, Washington

CHAPTER FIVE

Budget Analysts

A budget analyst works with a company, organization, government agency, or university to organize its finances, prepare financial reports, and oversee institutional spending. It's a job that is becoming more complex as new statistical techniques are being used to track, organize, and analyze financial data.

Duties and Job Responsibilities

Budget analysts have a wide range of job responsibilities. According to the U.S. Bureau of Labor Statistics, typical job duties include:

- Working with an organization's managers and department heads to develop an annual budget
- Reviewing budget proposals to ensure a comprehensive, complete, and accurate representation of a department's financial needs
- Ensuring budget proposals comply with appropriate laws and financial regulations

- Combining smaller department or project budgets into one large budget that represents the entire organization
- Reviewing requests for funding
- Monitoring overall spending to keep an organization within its budget

Budget analysts also offer their recommendations on funding requests; assist organizational leadership in understanding budget proposals and in identifying alternative methods of funding; and estimate and plan for future financial needs.

At times, bookkeeping and accounting professionals must give presentations to business leaders and executives.

Educational Requirements

A bachelor's degree in accounting or a related field is the most common preparation for entry into the budget analyst field. The position relies heavily on analytical and numerical skills, so degrees in economics, finance, business, or public administration are useful. Many employers prefer candidates who

Advanced mathematics, accounting, and business management skills can be developed through master's degrees in business administration, accounting, or finance.

have earned a master's degree in a subject area such as accounting, business administration, statistics, or mathematics.

The majority of budget analysts, more than 20 percent, work for state or federal governments. Budget analysts working in government jobs often earn the certified government financial manager credential, which covers the entire range of jobs in government

DOUGLAS W. ELMENDORF, CHIEF BUDGETING OFFICER, CONGRESSIONAL BUDGET OFFICE

"Making predictions is always difficult," Douglas W. Elmendorf said in a February 2010 interview with the *Fiscal Times*, a leading online news site dedicated to reporting the budgetary, financial, and economic issues facing the U.S government. Elmendorf serves the U.S. government as its chief budgeting officer. It's his job to assess the legislation politicians and lawmakers create and to hammer out the viability of a new initiative's budget. Elmendorf reviews and determines whether a proposal for extended health care coverage or a tax cut can survive financially.

As head of the Congressional Budget Office, Elmendorf's opinion on all aspects of the government budget can wield strong influence. He gained experience as a budget analyst for the Congressional Budget Office before becoming a senior economist at both the Federal Reserve Board and the White House Council of Economic Advisers. He earned a bachelor's degree in economics at Princeton University before attending Harvard University to earn a master's degree and a doctorate in economics. As part of his job, Elmendorf publishes dozens of reports and provides expert testimony before Congress and the House of Representatives on whether a legislative initiative is fiscally responsible.

financial management, at the local, state, and federal levels. To earn the certification, candidates must fulfill certain criteria, such as minimum levels of education and experience, plus they must pass a series of exams, which cover the governmental environment; government accounting, financial reporting, and budgeting; and government financial management and control. For more information, visit the Association of Government Accountants' website at http://www.agacgfm.org.

Budget analysts should also have strong communication skills as many must present their findings to others or distill information to those with little or no knowledge of budgets and the financial terminology commonly used by professionals in the field. Proficient public speaking skills are necessary to relay information in a clear and concise manner. Taking courses in communications, public speaking, or writing can strengthen your communication skills.

Career Outlook

The U.S. Bureau of Labor Statistics cites a 6 percent growth in budget analyst positions by 2022. As tax-paying citizens' concerns over public spending continue to rise, attention to budgets and spending will continue to be an important issue. As a result,

Anyone in the general public can scrutinize spending by government services since these services are funded with taxes paid by individuals.

budget analysts will be in demand as efficient use of public money is expected by both the public and by political leaders looking to strengthen the economy.

Advancement Opportunities

Entry-level budget analysts begin with a specific focus, such as a portion of an organization's budget, or a set of responsibilities that are part of a larger project. As they gain experience, more responsibility is awarded to them. Many budget analysts are promoted to intermediate or senior level positions, where they have more direct influence on the creation and execution of budgets and on the managing of an organization's spending. A master's degree in business administration, accounting, finance, or statistics can advance a budget analyst's skills and provide managerial and leadership training for higher-level positions.

CHAPTER SIX

Forensic Accountants

A forensic accountant is a special type of investigator that focuses on identifying fraudulent behavior in financial documents. This can include money laundering, embezzlement, locating hidden assets, bankruptcy and credit card fraud, falsifying insurance claims, and white-collar crime. A forensic accountant searches through complex financial statements and records to unearth any suspicious activity.

Forensic accountants seek out evidence of illegal financial crime. This can sometimes take years of work.

Duties and Job Responsibilities

Forensic accountants are accountants specifically trained to identify illegal financial activity. They conduct thorough forensic research and analysis of business and personal financial records in order to uncover the person, people, or organization responsible for committing a crime. They search through and analyze financial documents, statements, and records to identify and trace funds that have been moved illegally, and work to recover these assets. Forensic accountants also gather and present their evidence to law enforcement officials for search warrants and affidavits, they assist

GERVASE MACGREGOR, FCA, HEAD OF ADVISORY AND A SENIOR PARTNER, BDO

In an interview with TARGETJobs, Gervase MacGregor, described his role as a forensic accountant. "I investigate financial transactions with a view to explaining to a client where they've lost money, or to figure out what has happened and present evidence. My job is always about picking over the bones of something that has happened in the past—by the time a case is finished the event could be a decade or more in the past. For example, from 2001 to 2006 I worked on a big case involving events in the trucking industry at the end of the 1990s." MacGregor added advice for an accounting student interested in pursuing a career in the field: "I'd say go for it. But you need to make sure you have commercial understanding and, although it sounds obvious, you need an understanding of the basics of accounting. You have to enjoy digging and detective work, looking for evidence."

in interviewing witnesses and suspects to gather vital information about the suspected criminal activity, and they present their official findings at the conclusion of an investigation. If an investigation leads to arrests or prosecution, forensic accountants might meet with prosecuting attorneys to discuss their findings and could become expert witnesses in judicial proceedings.

Educational Requirements

A bachelor's or master's degree in forensic accounting, accounting, finance, or a related field is required to be a forensic accountant. In these programs, students complete a full gamut of accounting courses, in addition to course work that covers areas specific to forensic investigations, such as prevention and detection of fraudulent financial reporting, financial law, fraudulent schemes, financial statement fraud, criminology, litigation, and the legal system.

Multiple educational pathways can prepare you for a career as a forensic accountant. Certificate programs provide a basic introduction to the issues, principles, and practices involved in financial forensic investigation. These programs are for anyone with an interest in the field or in related careers such as attorneys and law enforcement professionals. A certificate alone will not prepare you for jobs in the field. However, coupled with a bachelor's or master's degree in a related field, it could provide you with the necessary skills needed for entry-level positions. The certificates, offered at the graduate and undergraduate levels, can help fulfill the

Forensic accountants often present and explain their findings in court. Their evidence is used to prove illegal criminal activity has occurred.

educational requirements needed for professional certifications in forensic accounting.

A bachelor's degree is the minimum level of education needed to enter the field. Many accounting programs offer concentrations or specializations in forensic accounting, which provide you with the investigative skills and knowledge needed for the field.

A master's degree in accounting, forensic accounting, or business administration can prepare you for the widest range of positions. These programs feature advanced level accounting, investigative, management, and leadership courses. They can take between twelve and twenty-four months to complete, depending on the program.

Professional Certifications

There are three professional certifications that forensic accountants can obtain. While certification is not required for practice in the field, most forensic accountants earn at least one certification to verify their knowledge and skills in the area.

The Certified in Financial Forensics (CFF) credential is for CPAs who work in forensic accounting. This certification demonstrates significant expertise in forensic accounting. Candidates must have a valid CPA license, have a minimum of one thousand hours of business experience in forensic accounting, possess seventy-five hours of professional continuing education in forensic accounting, and successfully pass the CFF exam. Among the exam topics are bankruptcy; computer forensic analysis; family law; and fraud prevention, detection, and response. The American Institute of Certified Public Accountants (AICPA) administers the exam.

The Certified Fraud Examiner certification credential tests your knowledge of the four major areas of fraud: fraud prevention and deterrence, financial transactions and fraud schemes, investigation, and law. Candidates must be an associate member of the Association of

Forensic accountants testiy on a wide range of topics, from bankruptcy, family law, and fraud, to financial schemes. They put their expertise to use in helping the justice system prosecute financial offenses.

Certified Fraud Examiners, hold a bachelor's degree, have at least two years of professional experience, and agree to the abide by the ACFE's Code of Professional Standards.

The Certified Forensic Accountant (Cr.FA) credential recognizes your skills, knowledge, experience, and commitment to the forensic accounting field. The exam is for CPAs. You must be a member of the

American College of Forensic Examiners Institute; hold a current CPA license; register with your state's board of accountancy; be compliant with all local, state, and federal regulations; and have no felony convictions. The American College of Forensic Examiners International offers the exam.

Career Outlook

The U.S. Bureau of Labor Statistics suggests a 22 percent growth in the field by 2018. Many of these positions will be in the private or nongovernment sector. The growth is due to changes in financial law, new government regulations affecting corporations, and the demand for greater accountability of spending.

Advancement Opportunities

Forensic accountants with a master's degree have the greatest opportunities for advancement. Leadership and management positions require someone with advanced knowledge of the field, plus the supervisory and managerial skills needed to oversee a staff. Long-term strategic planning also requires knowledge of business and operations. There are opportunities for advancement for those with bachelor's degrees, but without an advanced degree, earning potential and upward mobility will become limited.

CHAPTER SEVEN

Other Fascinating Financial Careers

A background in accounting and bookkeeping can prepare you for a wide range of careers beyond those directly associated with accounting and bookkeeping. Many exciting, dynamic careers are available to those with strong accounting, mathematics, computing, and business-related skills.

Accounting Information Systems Manager

Information systems managers are information technology (IT) experts and help an organization determine how computing, software, and technology can be used to organize, collect, and assess data. These professionals combine their knowledge of computing and IT with

Accounting information systems managers implement systems that make financial tasks easier.

accounting and management skills to create computing systems that support a wide range of needs specific to any company that deals with financial issues.

Commonly, accounting IT systems managers analyze an organization's computer, software, and hardware needs and make recommendations for upgrades or additional software. They install and upgrade hardware and software systems as necessary and determine which new technology initiatives are applicable to their organization. These positions also require overseeing the work of the entire IT staff, which can include computer systems analysts, software developers, information security analysts, and computer support specialists. Accounting IT systems managers also work with vendors to negotiate service and equipment contracts.

Most vital for accounting IT managers is the security and safety of an organization's networks, computing systems, and the information they contain. Retail companies, banks, universities, hospitals, and corporations all possess sensitive information that can range from Social Security numbers and bank account numbers to credit card numbers and health information. This data must be protected from the general public and kept secure.

Educational Requirements

You need a bachelor's degree that combines accounting and business knowledge with computing and information technology to become an accounting information systems manager. Some colleges and universities offer degrees in accounting information systems or

An accounting information systems professional must have extensive knowledge of both the fundamentals of accounting and of computing and information technology.

management information systems. These skills may also be obtained by earning a bachelor's degree in accounting and selecting a minor in information technology, management information systems, or computing security. Both pathways include course work in accounting and business plus courses in computing and information technology, database management systems, systems analysis and design, business technologies, programming, cyber security, networking, and systems administration.

Career Outlook and Advancement Opportunities

According to the U.S Bureau of Labor Statistics, computing and information systems managers, including accounting information systems managers, will experience a 15 percent growth in jobs by 2022. Many IT managers start out as lower level managers and advance to project or department managers. Those who are particularly business-minded may find themselves in leadership positions. A graduate degree can only support any ambitions to advance into management and leadership roles.

Hedge Fund Accountants

A hedge fund is an investment tool in which a small, limited group of investors participate. Hedge funds are run by professional management companies and, unlike other types of investments, such as stocks, they are private funds in which the general public cannot invest. Hedge funds invest their money in a wide range of markets or places, with the goal of making their initial investors a lot of money. The name refers to hedging techniques that are used to lessen the impact of any losses the fund could experience, which protects the investments made by the fund's participants.

Hedge fund accountants are experienced in dealing with the vast changes that occur in financial markets that can affect the value of a hedge fund. They create

UNCOMMON AND EXCITING ACCOUNTING CAREERS

- **Mergers and acquisitions accountant:** These accountants specialize in advising companies on adding a business to their portfolio, selling off divisions of a company, or merging with another firm.

- **Entertainment accountant:** Production budgets, payroll, and negotiating royalties on behalf of actors and writers are all functions of an entertainment accountant. Some of these accountants work directly for TV or film studios while others work for actors, directors, and producers.

- **Sports accountant:** These accountants negotiate salaries, manage a salary cap, monitor the profitability of an entire sports franchise, and are also responsible for keeping athletic teams' finances running smoothly. They oversee everything from players' salaries and trades, promotional events, merchandise, and operating budgets.

and manage investment portfolios that protect investors against losses. They research and analyze different types of investment opportunities and make investment recommendations. They also work with hedge fund managers who buy and sell investments for the fund.

Educational Requirements

A bachelor's degree in accounting is required for a hedge fund accountant position. Most hedge fund accountants also possess a master's degree in accounting or a master's of business administration (MBA). Many hedge fund accountants are also CPAs. They often are licensed securities traders through the Financial Industry Regulatory Authority, which is an organization that regulates the securities industry.

Career Outlook and Advancement Opportunities

The U.S. Bureau of Labor Statistics cites a 9 percent growth for all types of financial managers, including hedge fund managers, by 2020. As the economy grows, more financial managers will be needed to accommodate increases in services to those with an interest in investing their earnings. To advance in the field, a master's degree in accounting or business administration provides the education and preparation needed for positions in management and leadership.

Cost Estimators

A cost estimator is a professional who collects and analyzes data to help a company determine the time,

A cost estimator gathers information from engineers, contractors, and supply companies to determine if a new project is financially feasible.

money, materials, and labor required to manufacture a product, construct a building, or provide a service.

Cost estimators have a variety of responsibilities. They identify factors that affect the cost of a project, such as production time, supplies and materials, and labor expenses. By analyzing this information, they can prepare estimates that detail how much it will cost for an organization to take on a certain type of project. To gather this type of data, cost estimators work with engineers, architects, contractors, and supply companies. They review blueprints and technical documents, evaluate the profitability of a product or project, and develop plans to ensure the product or project can be manufactured or built on an efficient timetable.

Educational Requirements

A bachelor's degree is necessary for entry into the field. A background in mathematics is essential. Degrees in accounting or statistics, or degrees in areas where mathematics courses are a critical element of the curriculum, such as engineering or construction management, are often the most useful for the field. It also helps to have some knowledge of the industry in which you'd like to work. For product production, a degree in industrial engineering or business might be most helpful. For the construction industry, a degree in construction management or architecture would provide a strong educational background.

While certification is not a requirement, several organizations, including the American Society of Professional Estimators, the Association for the Advancement of Cost Estimating International, and the International Cost Estimating and Analysis Association, offer a variety of certifications in cost estimating and analysis.

Career Outlook and Advancement Opportunities

The field is expected to grow significantly by 2022. The U.S. Bureau of Labor Statistics projects a 26 percent increase in jobs for cost estimators. This growth is in response to an increase in accountability for how companies and government agencies use their money and to ensure that products are profitable for corporations. Growth in the construction industry will also fuel the need for more cost estimators.

CHAPTER EIGHT

Career Advancement in Bookkeeping and Accounting

Like all career fields, the accounting and bookkeeping industry has many exciting opportunities for advancement. These can include senior positions in the field as well as management and leadership positions where you can use your skills to help influence the direction of your organization or company. Advancement in the field can be dependent on an advanced degree, which can prepare you for a wide range of responsibilities in these upper-level positions.

Master's Degrees

A master's degree is an advanced degree beyond a bachelor's degree. It's a degree in which you immerse

Major companies, like Google, look for applicants who have studied for advanced degrees.

yourself in advanced-level courses in a particular area of study. For the accounting and bookkeeping fields, there are two main types of master's degrees.

MBA: Master of Business Administration

An MBA, or master of business administration, is an advanced business degree often pursued by those in the business, management, finance, or accounting fields. Most MBA programs begin with a set of required courses that cover common management topics, such as operations management, organizational leadership, teamwork and leadership, managerial economics, and financial analysis. MBA programs typically offer a wide range of concentrations, or focus areas, from which the student can choose based on career aspirations or interests. These can include accounting, finance, health care management, international business, management, leadership, management information systems, technology development, operations management, statistics, and more.

An MBA can range in length from one to two years depending on a student's choice of concentration and if the curriculum of your bachelor's degree included preparatory courses in certain areas of business.

MBA in Accounting

An MBA in accounting is a master's degree that combines the managerial aspects of an MBA degree with advanced course work in accounting. These programs cover topics such as financial accounting theory, competitive strategy, information systems auditing, cost management, and corporate valuation.

Graduate students in accounting are in demand. A recent study by the *Journal of Accountancy* showed that more than forty thousand new accounting graduates were hired in 2013 and more than sixty-one thousand accounting degrees, a third of them master's degrees, were awarded that same year.

A master of business administration (MBA) degree is among the most popular advanced degree options for people in accounting, bookkeeping, or finance careers.

TOP FIFTEEN COMPANIES THAT HIRE STUDENTS WITH AN MBA

1. Google, an Internet search engine
2. McKinsey & Company, a consulting firm
3. Apple, a software and product company
4. Bain & Company, a global management firm
5. Boston Consulting Group, a global management and business strategy firm
6. Amazon.com, a global online retailer
7. Goldman Sachs Group, an investment bank
8. Facebook, a social media corporation
9. Nike, a sports product corporation
10. JP Morgan, a global financial institution
11. Deloitte, an accounting and consulting corporation
12. Walt Disney, an entertainment corporation
13. IDEO, a design consultancy corporation
14. Blackstone Group, a global investment and advisory firm
15. Johnson & Johnson, a health care corporation

Doctorate Degree

A doctorate degree, the highest level and most intensive type of degree, qualifies a person to hold highly specialized positions in certain career fields, conduct high-level research on a particular subject, or pursue a teaching career at a college or university. A doctorate in accounting prepares you to conduct analytical research within the field, make changes in the regulatory structure of accounting, or influence the methods in which accountants gather and assess data.

The curriculum differs dramatically from a bachelor's or master's degree. Where these programs are focused more on addressing accounting principles and fundamental skills, doctorate programs focus on research about

A doctoral degree focuses more on the theory of financial and accounting principles than its practical application.

the accounting field. Courses emphasize knowledge of current and emerging research, as well as preparing students to conduct their own research. All doctoral degree candidates must write a thesis, which is a comprehensive research paper based on a topic the student chooses to study. Students spend several years conducting research before writing their thesis. Students also must present their thesis, as well as their research, to a group of experts who review and judge the work.

Licenses

As discussed in previous sections, the accounting and bookkeeping field is filled with opportunities to earn certifications that help support educational and experiential qualifications. Among the most common for the fields outlined in this book:

- Certified public accountant (CPA)
- Certified management accountant (CMA)
- Certified internal auditor (CIA)
- Certified information system auditor (CISA)
- Certified fraud examiner (CFE)
- Certified bank auditor (CBA)
- Certified government auditing professional (CGAP)

GLOSSARY

accounts payable The balance due to a creditor on a current account.

accounts receivable A balance due from a debtor on a current account.

acquisition The act of gaining an entity.

analyze To study something closely and carefully.

debt An amount of money that you owe to a person, bank, or company.

embezzlement Fradulent appropriation for one's own use.

expenditure An amount of money that is spent on something.

loss Money that is spent and that is more than the amount earned or received.

margin The difference that exists between net sales and the cost of merchandise sold and from which expenses are usually met or profit derived.

merger The act or process of combining two or more businesses into one business.

profit Money that is made in a business.

receipts Money that a business, bank, or government receives.

reconcile To make consistent.

revenue Money that is made by or paid to a business or an organization.

FOR MORE INFORMATION

American Accounting Association
5717 Bessie Drive
Sarasota, FL 34233-2399
(941) 921-7747
Website: http://www.aaahq.org
The American Accounting Association is the largest
community of accountants in academia. Founded
in 1916, it has a rich and reputable history built on
leading-edge research and publications.

American Institute of Professional Bookkeepers
6001 Montrose Road, Suite 500
Rockville, MD 20852
(800) 622-0121
Website: http://www.aipb.org
The American Institute of Professional Bookkeepers
was established in 1987 to recognize bookkeeping
as a profession and bookkeepers as professionals.

Association of Chartered Certified Accountants
84 Great Suffolk Street
London SE1 0BE
England
Website: http://www.accacareers.com
ACCA is the global body for professional accountants
with more than half a million students and members
in two hundred countries.

Association of Government Accountants
2208 Mount Vernon Avenue
Alexandria, VA 22301
(800) 242-7211

Website: http://www.agacgfm.org
This is a member organization for financial professionals in government.

National Association of Certified Public Bookkeepers
Station Park
140 N. Union Avenue, Suite 240
Farmington, UT 84025
(866) 444-9989
Website: http://www.nacpb.org
NACPB is the only national bookkeeping association dedicated exclusively to the needs of bookkeeping professionals providing bookkeeping services to the public.

National Society of Accountants
1010 N. Fairfax Street
Alexandria, VA 22314
(800) 966-6679
Website: http://www.nsacct.org
NSA provides national leadership and helps its members
achieve success in the profession of accountancy
and taxation through the advocacy of practice rights
and the promotion of high standards in ethics, education, and professional excellence.

Websites

Because of the changing nature of Internet links, Rosen
Publishing has developed an online list of websites
related to the subject of this book. This site is updated
regularly. Please use this link to access the list:

http://www.rosenlinks.com/RDFM/Book

FOR FURTHER READING

Berger, Lauren. *All Work, No Pay: Finding an Internship, Building Your Resume, Making Connections, and Gaining Job Experience*. New York, NY: Ten Speed Press, 2012.

Berger, Sandra. *The Ultimate Guide to Summer Opportunities for Teens: 200 Programs That Prepare You for College Success*. Waco, TX: Prufrock Press, 2007.

Bernstein, Daryl, and Rob Husberg. *Better Than a Lemonade Stand!: Small Business Ideas for Kids*. New York, NY: Aladdin/Beyond Words, 2012.

Bochner, Arthur, Rose Bochner, and Adriane G. Berg. *New Totally Awesome Business Books for Kids*. New York, NY: William Morrow Paperbacks, 2007.

Christen, Carol, and Richard N. Bolles. *What Color Is Your Parachute? For Teens*. New York, NY: Ten Speed Press, 2010.

Gulko, Candace S. *Field Guides to Finding a New Career: Accounting, Business, and Finance*. New York, NY: Ferguson Publishing Company, 2010.

Kiyosaki, Robert T. *Rich Dad Poor Dad for Teens: The Secrets About Money That You Don't Learn in School*. Scottsdale, AZ: Plata Publishing, 2012.

Lore, Nicholas. *Now What?: The Young Person's Guide to Choosing the Perfect Career*. New York, NY: Touchstone, 2008.

Lyden, Mark. *College Students: Do This! Get Hired!* BookSurge Publishing, 2009.

Maybury, Richard J. *Whatever Happened to Penny Candy? A Fast, Clear, and Fun Explanation of the Economics*

You Need for Success in Your Career, Business, and Investments. Placerville, CA: Bluestocking, 2010.

Meyer, Susan. *Careers as a Bookkeeper and Auditor*. New York, NY: Rosen Publishing Group, 2014.

Pollak, Lindsey. *Getting from College to Career: Your Essential Guide to Succeeding in the Real World*. New York, NY: HarperBusiness, 2012.

Rainer, R. Kelly, Efraim Turban, Ingrid Splettstoesser-Hogeterp, and Cristobal Sanchez-Rodriguez. *Introduction to Information Systems: Supporting and Transforming Business*. Indianapolis, IN: Wiley Publishing, 2008.

Reber, Deborah, and Lisa Fyfe. *In Their Shoes: Extraordinary Women Describe Their Amazing Careers*. New York, NY: Simon Pulse, 2007.

Seupel, Celia W. *Top Careers in Two Years: Business, Finance and Government Administration*. New York, NY: Ferguson Publishing Company, 2007.

Toren, Adam, and Matthew Toren. *Kidpreneurs: Young Entrepreneurs with Big Ideas!* Phoenix, AZ: Business Plus Media Group LLC, 2009.

Williams, Jane A. *A Bluestocking Guide: Economics*. Placerville, CA: Bluestocking, 2010.

BIBLIOGRAPHY

American Institute of CPAs. "Become a CPA." Retrieved January 28, 2014 (http://www.aicpa.org/BecomeACPA/Pages/BecomeaCPA.aspx).

American Institute of CPAs. "Certified in Financial Forensics (CFF) Credential Overview." Retrieved January 29, 2014 (http://www.aicpa.org).

American Institute of Professional Bookkeepers. "Certified Bookkeeper Certification." Retrieved January 28, 2014 (http://www.aipb.org/certification_program.htm).

Association of Certified Fraud Examiners. "Forensic Accountant." Retrieved January 29, 2014 (http://www.acfe.com/career-path-forensic-accountant.aspx).

Association of Certified Fraud Examiners. "Government Accounting." Retrieved January 22, 2014 (http://www.acfe.com).

Association of Certified Fraud Examiners. "How to Become a CFE." Retrieved January 29, 2014 (http://www.acfe.com/become-cfe-qualifications.aspx).

Association of Certified Fraud Examiners. "Public Accountant." Retrieved January 22, 2014 (http://www.acfe.com).

Association of Government Accountants. "Certified Government Financial Manager." Retrieved January 29, 2014 (http://www.agacgfm.org).

Berger, Lauren. *All Work, No Pay: Finding an Internship, Building Your Resume, Making Connections, and Gaining Job Experience*. Berkeley, CA: Ten Speed Press, 2012.

Chambers, Erin. "Tips to Make the Most of Summer Internships." *Wall Street Journal*, July 1, 2008. Retrieved January 27, 2014 (http://online.wsj.com).

CNN Money. "Top 15 MBA Employers." June 5, 2012. Retrieved January 30, 2014 (http://money.cnn.com).

Colleges and Degrees. "Job Outlook for the Field of Forensic Accounting." Retrieved January 30, 2014 (http://www.collegesanddegrees.com).

Cunningham, Andrew. "iPad Air Profit Margins Reportedly Range from 45 to 61 Percent." Ars Technica, November 5, 2013. Retrieved January 22, 2014 (http://arstechnica.com).

Drew. Jill. "Low Profile, High Impact: Congressional Budget Office Director Doug Elmendorf." *Fiscal Times*, February 11, 2010. Retrieved January 29, 2014 (http://www.thefiscaltimes.com).

EZine Articles. "Associate's Degrees Vs. Bachelor's Degrees." Retrieved January 24, 2014 (http://ezinearticles.com).

Forensic Accounting. "Studying Forensic Accounting." Retrieved January 29, 2014 (http://www.forensicaccounting.net/#).

Institute of Internal Auditors. "Certified Internal Auditor." Retrieved January 28, 2014 (na.theiia.org).

Liang, Jengyee. *Hello Real World!: A Student's Approach to Great Internships, Co-Ops, and Entry Level Positions*. BookSurge Publishing, 2006.

National Association of Certified Public Bookkeepers. "Certified Payroll Specialist License." Retrieved January 28, 2014 (http://www.nacpb.org/licenses/cps.cfm).

National Bookkeepers Association. "Membership." Retrieved January 28, 2014 (http://www.national ba.org/membership.cfm).

National Bookkeepers Association. "Microsoft Excel Certification." Retrieved January 28, 2014 (http:// www.nationalba.org/certification/microsoft-excel -certification.cfm).

North Carolina State University: Industrial Extension Service. "Pros and Cons of an Online Education." October 2010. Retrieved January 24, 2014 (http:// www.ies.ncsu.edu).

North Seattle College. "Bookkeeping Certificate in Accounting." Retrieved January 22, 2014 (https:// northseattle.edu/certificates/bookkeeping -certificate-accounting).

Ross, Stan, and James Carberry. *The Inside Track to Careers in Accounting*. New York, NY: AICPA, 2010.

Thomson, Jeff. "CFO at 28: Career Advice from a Seasoned Professional." Forbes.com, September 7, 2012. Retrieved January 29, 2014 (http://www .forbes.com).

University of Phoenix. "Review Tuition and Expenses." Retrieved January 24, 2014 (https://www .phoenix.edu).

U.S. Bureau of Labor Statistics. "Bookkeeping, Accounting, and Auditing Clerks." January 8, 2014. Retrieved January 21, 2014 (http://www.bls.gov).

U.S. Bureau of Labor Statistics. "Budget Analyst." January 8, 2014. Retrieved January 27, 2014 (http://www.bls.gov).

U.S. Bureau of Labor Statistics. "Computer and
Information Systems Managers." January 8, 2014.
Retrieved January 30, 2014 (http://www.bls.gov).

U.S. Bureau of Labor Statistics. "Cost Estimators."
January 8, 2014. Retrieved January 21, 2014
(http://www.bls.gov).

U.S. Bureau of Labor Statistics. "Financial Managers."
January 8, 2014. Retrieved January 30, 2014
(http://www.bls.gov).

U.S. News & World Report. "Bookkeeping, Auditing and
Accounting Clerk." Retrieved January 28, 2014
(http://money.usnews.com/careers/best-jobs/
bookeeping-accouting-and-audit-clerk).

U.S. News & World Report. "University of Pennsylvania." Retrieved January 24, 2014 (http://colleges
.usnews.rankingsandreviews.com/best-colleges/
university-of-pennsylvania-3378).

Zupek, Rachel. "Top 10 Jobs in Accounting." Mywizjobs
.com. Retrieved January 27, 2014 (http://www
.mywizjobs.com).

INDEX

About the Author

Laura La Bella is the author of more than twenty-five nonfiction children's books. Among other titles, she has written numerous books on economics as well as career and work readiness guides, including *Careers in Web Development*, *Careers in Crisis Management and Hostage Negotiation*, *Internship and Volunteer Opportunities for People Who Love to Build Things*, *Dream Jobs in Sports Fitness and Medicine*, *How Consumer Credit and Debt Work*, *How Commodity Trading Works*, *How Taxation Works*, and *World Financial Meltdown*. La Bella lives in Rochester, New York, with her husband and son.

Photo Credits

Cover (figure) Bevan Goldswain/Shutterstock.com; cover (background) Kekyalyaynen/Shutterstock.com; back cover, pp. 7, 15 (top), 26 (top), 34, 40, 46 (top), 53 (top), 61 (top) YanLev/Shutterstock.com; p. 1 Andrey Popov/Shutterstock.com; pp. 4–5 (background) hxdbzxy/Shutterstock.com; p. 5 Cheryl Savan/Shutterstock.com; pp. 8, 17 wavebreakmedia/Shutterstock.com; p. 9 Shutter_M/Shutterstock.com; p. 13 David Sachs/Digital Vision/Thinkstock; pp. 15, 59 Goodluz/Shutterstock.com; pp. 22, 32 monkeybusineeeimages/iStock/Thinkstock; p. 26 PathDoc/Shutterstock.com; p. 28 © Institute of Management Accountants; p. 35 Digital Vision/Photodisc/Thinkstock; p. 38 gary718/Shutterstock.com; pp. 41, 55 Monkey Business Images/Shutterstock.com; p. 42 racorn/Shutterstock.com; p. 44 westlaker/Shutterstock.com; p. 46 James Lauritz/Photodisc/Getty Images; p. 49 bikeriderlondon/Shutterstock.com; p. 51 Fuse/Thinkstock; p. 53 PhotoAlto/Eric Audras/Brand X Pictures/Getty Images; p. 61 Universal Images Group/SuperStock; p. 63 michaeljung/iStock/Thinkstock; p. 65 Liushengfilm/Shutterstock.com; additional cover and interior design elements PremiumVector/Shutterstock.com, Mike McDonald/Shutterstock.com (emblem components), Milena_Bo/Shutterstock.com, ririro/Shutterstock.com, The_Pixel/Shutterstock.com, Zffoto/Shutterstock.com, Rafal Olechowski/Shutterstock.com (banners, backgrounds).

Designer: Michael Moy; Editor: Tracey Baptiste; Photo Researcher: Marty Levick